6/2003

BASKETBALL

FOR FUN!

By Brian Eule

Content Adviser: Clay Weiner, Writer and Player/Coach, Brooklyn, New York
Reading Adviser: Frances J. Bonacci, Reading Specialist, Cambridge, Massachusetts

COMPASS POINT BOOKS

MINNEAPOLIS, MINNESOTA

Compass Point Books
3109 West 50th Street, #115
Minneapolis, MN 55410

Visit Compass Point Books on the Internet at *www.compasspointbooks.com*
or e-mail your request to *custserv@compasspointbooks.com*

Editors: Ryan Blitstein/Bill SMITH STUDIO and Catherine Neitge
Photo Researchers: Christie Silver and Sandra Will/Bill SMITH STUDIO
Designer: Jay Jaffe/Bill SMITH STUDIO

Library of Congress Cataloging-in-Publication Data
Eule, Brian.
    Basketball for fun / by Brian Eule.
        p. cm. — (Sports for fun)
    Summary: Describes the basic rules, skills, and important people and events in the sport of basketball.
    Includes bibliographical references (p.   ) and index.
    ISBN 0-7565-0429-5 (hardcover)
    1. Basketball—Juvenile literature. [1. Basketball.] I. Title. II. Series.
    GV885.1.E85 2003
    797.323—dc21   2002015115

Table of Contents

Ground Rules

Playing the Game

People, Places, and Fun

Note: In this book, there are two kinds of vocabulary words. Basketball Words to Know are words specific to basketball. They are in **bold** and are defined on page 46. Other Words to Know are helpful words that aren't related only to basketball. They are in ***bold and italicized***. These are defined on page 47.

In the Basket

Dr. James Naismith didn't know what to do. It was 1891, it was winter, and it was cold. He was a gym teacher at a school in Springfield, Massachusetts. Naismith had to come up with a game that could be played indoors.

He hung two peach baskets from the gym's balcony, ten feet [three meters] above the floor. Then, he put students into two teams. The students tried to throw a soccer ball into the baskets. Over 100 years later, this game, which we call "basketball," is one of the most popular sports in the world.

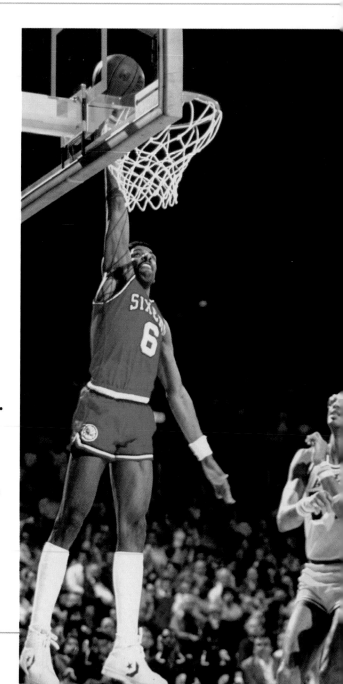

Through the Hoop

The goal of the game is to score as many points as possible. Teams score points by throwing the ball through the hoop for a **field goal**. The defense tries to stop the other team from scoring by taking the ball away.

*In the NBA and NCAA, the basketball is about thirty inches [seventy-six centimeters] around. The WNBA and kids' leagues use a smaller ball. When they are **inflated**, NBA balls weigh a little more than a pound [0.45 kilograms].*

On the Court

The height of the basket is ten feet (three meters). The rim of the basket has a hole in it. This is why the basket is sometimes called a hoop. Attached to the back of the rim is a backboard in the shape of either a rectangle or fan.

Courts are ninety-four feet [twenty-nine meters] long and fifty feet [fifteen meters] wide. Outlining the court are four lines. The two long ones are **sidelines** and the short ones are **endlines**. A line nineteen feet [six meters] out from the endline is called the **free-throw line**. It connects two lines that make up the lane. The three-point arc is the huge semicircle that stretches to the edge of the court and goes around the lane. The midcourt line divides the basketball court into two halves. Look at the picture to learn the names of the parts of the basketball court.

backboard

basket

sideline

free-throw line

three-point arc

lane

endline

Starting Lineup

Each team must have five players on the court. These five players play offense when their team has the ball. They also play defense when the other team has the ball. Each team scores in one basket and defends the other. The players have to run back and forth between the two baskets. Basketball is a very fast game!

Both teams have a coach on the bench on the sidelines. The coach may call out ideas for plays. He or she might point out something that the players did not notice. Also sitting on the bench are reserve players. They come into the game when the starters get tired.

Shoot to Score

Scoring points in basketball is simple. Put the ball through the hoop. This is called a field goal. Most field goals are worth two points. A shot from beyond the three-point arc is a three-pointer. It's worth (you guessed it) three points.

From Downtown!

The three-point shot wasn't created until seventy years after the first basketball game. The American Basketball Association (ABA) added it to make games more exciting. Three-point shots are now used in both professional and college basketball. If a team is down by two points with only a second left, they can win the game with one long shot.

TYPE OF SHOT	POINTS
Free Throw	1
Field Goal	2
Field Goal behind three-point line	3

In college basketball the three-point line is closer than in the pros.

three-point line

Suiting Up

Finding comfortable shoes is very important. Playing basketball involves a lot of running and jumping. Most basketball players wear high-top shoes because they support the ankles.

Many players who wear glasses off the court wear safety goggles during games to protect their eyes.

The basketball uniform has a jersey (shirt) and shorts. About twenty years ago, these shorts were very short! Now they usually go down to the knees.

Many basketball players also wear a mouthpiece to protect their teeth from flying elbows.

Basketball players wear light shoes so they can run and jump on the court. Most players wear high-tops so they don't sprain an ankle.

Tip-off

Every game begins with a tip-off called a **jump ball**. One player from each team stands at the midcourt line. Around this line is a circle. The other players gather around this circle.

The **referee** throws the ball straight up between the two players. They are not allowed to grab the ball themselves. They each try to tip it to a teammate. The players in the tip-off are usually very tall. They can also jump several feet in the air!

How's the Weather Up There?

The tallest players ever to play in the NBA were Gheorghe Muresan and Manute Bol. They were both measured at 7 feet and 7 inches [2.3 m]. Above, Bol stands next to Washington Bullets teammate Muggsy Bogues, who is 5 feet and 3 inches [1.6 m].

On the Offense

Each team has five players on the court. Two are guards, two are forwards, and one is a center. When any of these players has the ball, the team is on offense.

- **Guards:** These players stand the farthest from the basket. They are usually smaller and faster than their teammates. They are also good at **dribbling** (see p. 20) and passing the ball. One of the guards is called the point guard. He or she brings the ball down the court and sets up the plays. The other guard is called the shooting guard. He or she must shoot well from long distances.

- **Forwards:** These players are a little taller than the guards. Forwards stand closer to the basket. They need to be good shooters, but they also have to use their height to **rebound**. Rebounding is grabbing the ball as it comes off the basket after a missed shot. The power forward is usually a little bigger. The other forward is the small forward.

- **Center:** This is the tallest player on the team. He or she usually stands under the basket as much as possible for short shots and lots of rebounds.

De-fense! De-fense!

When the other team has the ball, it's time for defense. The defense must stop the other team from scoring.

In the Zone

There are many different ways for a team to play defense. In **man-to-man** defense, each defensive player guards (defends) one offensive player. Guards usually defend guards, forwards defend forwards, and centers defend centers. In **zone** defense, each defensive player defends one part of the court. Players usually defend the same spots on the court where they stand on offense.

STEALING	**A defensive player takes the ball away from an offensive player.**
BLOCKING	**A defensive player blocks a pass or shot by an offensive player.**
MAKING THE OFFENSE MISS	**The defensive players guard the offense tight. The offensive player has to take a tough shot, which they'll usually miss.**

Moving the Ball

Basketball players can't just carry the ball. They have to dribble it. They bounce it up and down while they are moving. If a player walks without dribbling, he or she will be called for **traveling**. Because of this penalty, the other team gets the ball.

The other way to move the ball is to pass it from one player to another. There are many ways to pass the ball. In a bounce pass, a player bounces the ball off the ground to a teammate. In a chest pass, a player pushes the ball straight from the chest.

When a player scores after receiving a pass, the passer is given an **assist**.

Pass it Along!
John Stockton of the Utah Jazz has over 15,000 assists. That's more than any player in NBA history.

Big Shot

There are many ways to shoot the ball.

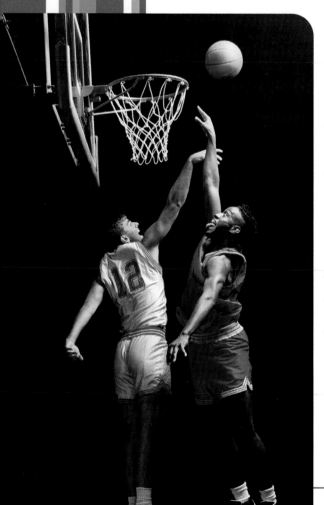

The easiest shot is the **lay-up**. It's a one-handed shot from close to the hoop. Most players bounce the ball off the backboard in a lay-up.

The **jump shot** is the most common shot. The player jumps up and shoots the ball in midair. Players use the strength from their legs to push the ball. The jump shot can go long distances.

A tougher shot to make is the **hook shot**. The player throws the ball high into the air by swinging one arm over the head. The hook shot is almost never blocked. Be careful, though. The hook shot is hard to control!

The Dunking Doctor

An exciting way to score is the **slam dunk**. Players jump up to the rim and slam the ball through the hoop. Julius Erving, whose nickname is "Dr. J," was one of the first great dunkers. Dr. J would glide through the air and slam the ball into the basket. His dunks were from as far as the free-throw line.

Give It a Shot!

Players shooting the ball must be comfortable with their **stance**. They face the basket with feet apart and bent knees.

1. A player should bend the elbows without sticking them out to the side. He or she keeps them tucked into the body.

2. Right-handed players bend their right wrist back and put the basketball into the right palm. The hand should be on the bottom and back side of the ball.

3. Place the left hand on the side of the ball for support. For lefties, it's the opposite.

4. In one motion, the shooter straightens the legs and arms while pushing the shooting arm up into the air.

5. A flick of the wrist lets the ball roll off the fingertips.

It helps if players think of themselves as a spring. By bending the knees, they are pushing the spring down. When they straighten up, all of this power goes into the shot.

Playing D

Defense is played with the hands out. This makes it harder for the offensive player to see the court. It also helps the defensive player steal and block. The arms should not be straight up in the air. Keep the elbows bent slightly. Raise the arms above the waist and out to the side. The hands should follow the ball. If the ball is held high, the defender's hands should be a little higher. If the ball is held low, the defender's hands should be a little lower.

Keeping the knees bent is also important. This helps the defender to be ready for anything—a pass, a shot, or dribbling. To move to the side quickly, the defender slides or shuffles the feet. Crossing one leg over the other slows the defender down.

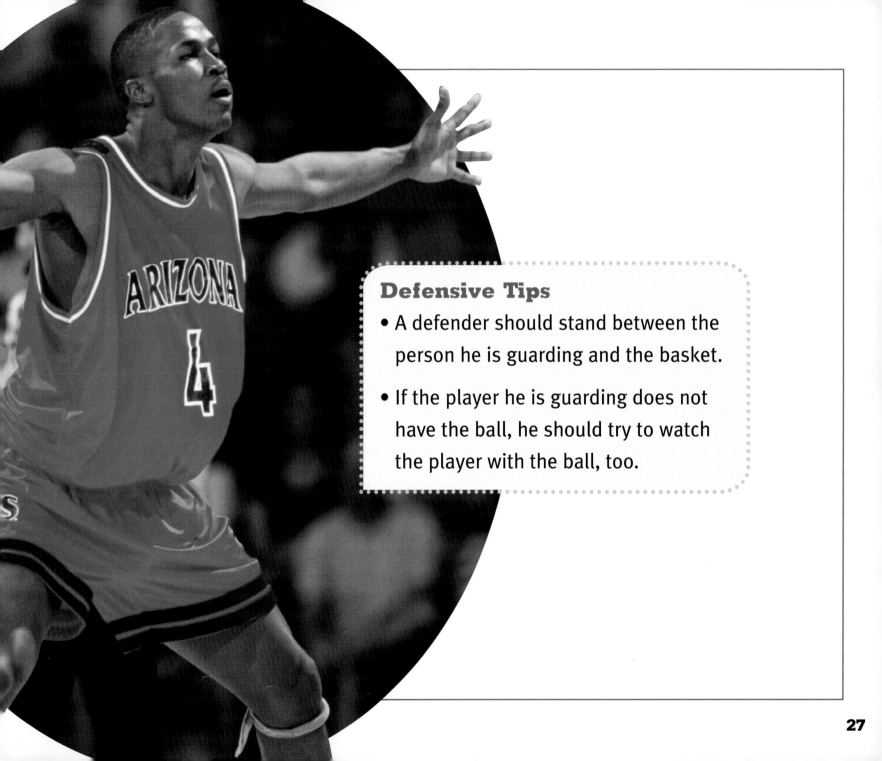

Defensive Tips

- A defender should stand between the person he is guarding and the basket.

- If the player he is guarding does not have the ball, he should try to watch the player with the ball, too.

Grab That Rebound

It's always important to get rebounds. On offense, a team can get a second chance at scoring after a missed basket. The defensive team gets rebounds to stop the offense from getting that second chance. The team with more rebounds has a better chance of winning the game.

Rebounding is not just about jumping for the ball. Good rebounders jump at the right time from the right place. They also **box out** their opponents. This means that they keep themselves between their opponent and the basket.

Another thing to remember about rebounding is to use two hands. This will help control the ball. Otherwise, the ball will be tipped away to another player.

Something Is Foul

There are two types of fouls in basketball: personal fouls and technical fouls. A referee signals a foul by blowing a whistle.

If a defensive player swats at the ball but hits the opponent's arm instead, it is a personal foul. Personal fouls can be called anytime there is *illegal* contact on the court. In the NBA and WNBA, when players have six fouls, they must sit out the rest of the game. In college, it only takes five to foul out.

Technical fouls are called for arguing, fighting, or using bad words. Technical fouls don't happen as often. It only takes two to be kicked out of the game.

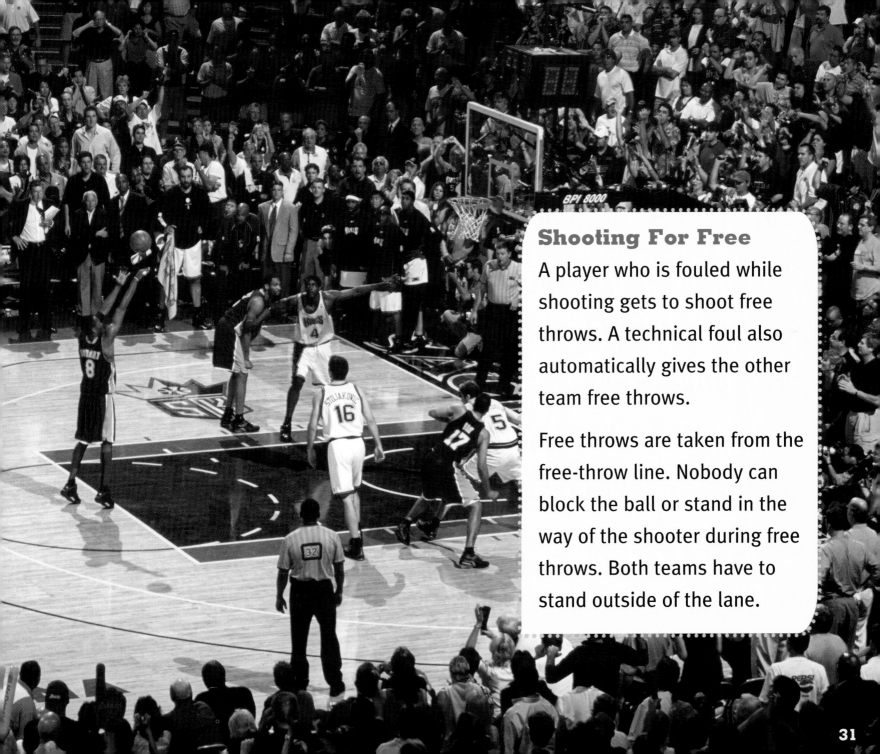

Shooting For Free

A player who is fouled while shooting gets to shoot free throws. A technical foul also automatically gives the other team free throws.

Free throws are taken from the free-throw line. Nobody can block the ball or stand in the way of the shooter during free throws. Both teams have to stand outside of the lane.

The Rule Book

Rules are an important part of basketball. Without them, teams wouldn't know when the game was over or when a basket counted. Here are some rules that help make the game easier to understand:

- Each NBA game has four twelve-minute periods called quarters.

- WNBA and college games have two twenty-minute halves.

- A small clock called the **shot clock** sits above the backboard. It counts how much time is left before the offense must shoot the ball. The shot clock is set for thirty-five seconds for college men, thirty seconds for college women and the WNBA, and twenty-four seconds in the NBA. If the shot clock hits zero and the player hasn't taken a shot, the other team gets the ball.

- If a player bounces or throws the ball outside of the court, it is out of bounds. The ball then goes to the other team.

- A player cannot stop dribbling, hold the ball, and start dribbling again. The player must pass or shoot after picking up the dribble. If the player doesn't, it's called a double dribble and the ball goes to the other team.

Timeout!

Teams can stop the game with a timeout. The team gathers around the bench to hear what the coach has to say. The coach might *diagram* plays or put in reserve players.

The coach's job is to *strategize.* He or she must answer questions. Who should play center? Should the defense be zone or man-to-man?

If one player is scoring really well for the other team, the coach might suggest **double-teaming** this player. Two defenders will guard that player.

A Fun Job

The timeout is also a way for the players to rest from the fast, tiring game. In the professional leagues, there are kids who bring the players water and towels during timeouts. These **ballboys** and **ballgirls** are hired by the team.

Getting Paid to Play

Professional basketball means that the players are paid money to play the game. The first "pro" game was held in Trenton, New Jersey, in 1896. The players were paid $15 each. There wasn't a nationwide basketball league back then. There were many smaller leagues.

In 1949, two of the smaller leagues joined forces. The National Basketball League and the Basketball Association of America combined to form the NBA.

Today, the NBA has twenty-nine teams. NBA games are watched throughout the world. But it isn't the only place to see professional basketball. The United States has a women's league, the WNBA, with sixteen teams.

There is also a new National Basketball Development League (NBDL) with eight teams.

Basketball Everywhere!

Basketball is played all over the world. There are professional basketball leagues in many places including Europe, Asia, the Middle East, and Canada.

Croatian superstar Toni Kukoc, at left, joined the NBA in 1993.

Legends

Basketball has had many great players and coaches. John Wooden and Michael Jordan are two of the game's best.

John Wooden

John Wooden is called the **"*Wizard* of Westwood"** for his coaching skills. Before he was a great coach, he was a great player, too. Wooden was born in Martinsville, Indiana, on October 14, 1910. He led Purdue University to the National Championship in 1932 and was named college basketball's player of the year. He went on to coach the UCLA Bruins. Wooden's teams won the NCAA Championship a record ten times. He was named coach of the year six times. Over a period of four seasons, Wooden's UCLA teams won eighty-eight straight games!

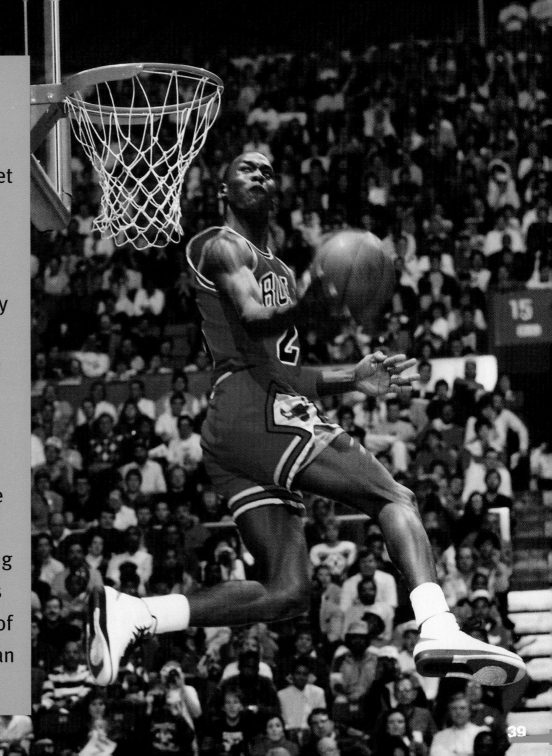

Michael Jordan

As a sophomore in high school, Michael Jordan didn't make his school's basketball team. He didn't let that stop him. Jordan practiced for hours every day. He became what many call the greatest basketball player ever. Jordan was born February 17, 1963, in Brooklyn, New York. In college, he scored the game-winning shot for North Carolina in the 1982 NCAA Championship. Jordan went on to win six NBA Championships with the Chicago Bulls. He was named the league's most valuable player (MVP) five times. Jordan is known for playing both strong offense and defense. His great jumping ability made him one of the game's great slam dunkers. Jordan is now with the Washington Wizards.

The Big Games

There are certain times when basketball fans get really excited. One of them is the NBA Finals. The Finals take place at the end of the NBA playoffs every June. The best teams from the Eastern and Western Conferences play in a best-of-seven series. That means the first team to win four games is crowned NBA Champion. The WNBA teams meet later in the summer for a best-of-three series.

March Madness

The NCAA tournament earned the nickname "March Madness" because basketball fans get so excited for it every March. The tournament began in 1939 with just eight college teams. Now, sixty-four schools compete for the chance to go to the "Final Four." That's the place where the four best teams go to play the tournament's semifinal and final games.

There is a men's tournament and a women's tournament. Both of them are **single elimination tournaments**. That means one loss ends a team's season.

Perfection!

In 2002, the University of Connecticut women won their tournament to cap off a perfect season. They had 39 victories and not one loss!

What Happened When?

1890　　1900　　1910　　1930　　1940

1891 Dr. James Naismith *invents* the game of basketball.

1895 The first backboards are attached to stop fans on balconies from reaching over and helping their teams.

1897 Yale defeats Penn in the first college game with teams of five players.

1898 The National Basketball League, the first pro league, is formed in New Jersey and Pennsylvania.

1902 Harry "Bucky" Lew is the first African-American to play in a white basketball league.

1906 Baskets with holes in the bottom are introduced.

1934 The first college basketball **doubleheader** is held at Madison Square Garden in front of more than 16,000 fans.

1936 Men's basketball becomes an Olympic sport.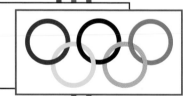

1938 The first college tournament, called the National Invitational Tournament (NIT), is played.

1939 Oregon wins the first NCAA men's basketball tournament.

James Naismith

1950 **1960** **1970** **1980** **1990** **2000**

1947 The Philadelphia Warriors win the first Basketball Association of America title.

1949 The NBA is formed.

1954 NBA introduces the 24-second clock.

1960 Danny Heater of Burnsville, West Virginia, scores 135 points in a boys' high school game.

1962 Wilt Chamberlain scores 100 points in an NBA game between the Warriors and the Knicks.

1964 UCLA wins the first of its record eleven national championships in men's basketball.

1976 Women's basketball becomes an Olympic sport.

1979 The NBA adds the three-point field goal.

1982 Louisiana Tech wins the first NCAA women's basketball tournament.

1982 Cheryl Miller of Riverside, California, scores 105 points in a girls' high school game.

1992 The U.S. Olympic "Dream Team" men's team wins the gold medal.

1997–2000 The Houston Comets win the first four WNBA Championships. Cynthia Cooper is named the Finals MVP all four times.

◄ *Wilt Chamberlain*

Cynthia Cooper ►

43

Basketball Bonanza

Most team names end in the letter **s**, but there are three teams in the NBA that don't. They are the Miami Heat, the Orlando Magic, and the Utah Jazz.

Kareem Abdul-Jabbar scored the most points of any player in NBA history. He scored 38,387 points in twenty NBA seasons. The most points scored in one game by one player was by Wilt "The Stilt" Chamberlain. He scored 100 points for the Philadelphia 76ers on March 2, 1962.

The most points an NBA team has ever scored in a game is 186 by the Detroit Pistons. They did it in a triple-overtime game against the Denver Nuggets in 1983. The second most? It is 184 by the Nuggets in the same game.

Basketball players are sometimes called cagers because a wire mesh cage used to surround some of the courts in the first pro games. The cages separated the players and the fans.

PISTONS TIME NUGGETS
186 00:00 184

The Harlem Globetrotters travel around the world for their games. They almost never lose. From 1971 to 1995 they had 8,829 straight wins! The Globetrotters have a lot of fun on the court. They spin the ball on one finger or make a pass between an opponent's legs. The team also helped invent special plays like the slam dunk. Many of the NBA's best players got their start with the Globetrotters.

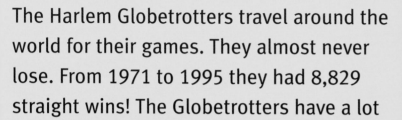

The official NBA logo is the silhouette of former Laker great Jerry West.

A finger-roll may sound like a dessert, but actually it's a way to shoot. A player shoots the ball underhand, letting it roll off the fingertips near the basket.

Basketball Words to Know

assist: the statistic given to the passer when a player scores after receiving a pass

ballboys/ballgirls: kids hired by professional teams to give water and towels to players and to retrieve basketballs

box out: to position oneself between the basket and an opponent in an attempt to grab a rebound

doubleheader: two games played the same day, one right after another

double-teaming: two defenders guarding one offensive player

dribble: to bounce the ball; the only way to move with the basketball

endlines: the two lines on the short sides of the rectangular basketball court; also called baselines, they are underneath the two baskets

field goal: a successful shot taken from the court while the game is in play; if shot from in front of the three-point line, these are worth two points; if shot from behind the three-point line, these are worth three points

free-throw line: a line nineteen feet out from the endline; where players go to shoot the foul shots called free throws

hook shot: a way of shooting the ball by swinging one arm over the head

jump ball: when two players stand opposite each other, jumping to tip a ball thrown in the air by a referee standing between them; the way a basketball game begins; also used when two players both have possession of the ball at the same time

jump shot: a shot taken while jumping

lay-up: an easy shot taken from very close range; a one-handed shot usually gently banked off the backboard

man-to-man: a type of defense in which each player is responsible for defending one person

NBA: the National Basketball Association

NBDL: the National Basketball Development League

NCAA: the National Collegiate Athletic Association, which runs college basketball

offense: the team in possession of the ball

rebound: a missed shot that bounces off the basket or backboard

referee: an official on the basketball court

shot clock: the clock that determines how much time before a team must shoot; usually above the backboard; resets when a shot hits the rim or when the other team gets possession of the ball

sidelines: the two long lines on either side of the basketball court

single elimination tournament: tournament in which one loss will end a team's run

slam dunk: a player jumps up to the rim and slams the ball through the hoop

traveling: a violation in basketball when a player takes steps without dribbling

WNBA: the Women's National Basketball Association

zone: a type of defense in which each player is responsible for defending an area of the court

Metric Conversion
1 foot = .3048 meters

Other Words to Know

Here are definitions of some of the words used in this book:

consist: to be made up of

diagram: a drawing that helps people understand something

inflate: to blow up with air

illegal: against the rules

invent: to create something and be the first to make it

professional: a person paid to do a job or play a game

substitute: a person or thing that replaces another person or thing

stance: the way a person is standing

strategize: to spend time thinking about ways to do something

wizard: a magician or person with special skills and powers

Where To Learn More

AT THE LIBRARY

Gaitley, Stephanie. (ed.) *Five-Star Girls' Basketball Drills*. Terre Haute, Ind.: Wish Publishing, 2000.

Marcus, Howard. *Basketball Basics*. New York: McGraw-Hill/Contemporary Books, 1991.

Paye, Burrall, and Patrick Paye. *Youth Basketball Drills*. Champaign, Ill.: Human Kinetics, 2000.

ON THE ROAD

NCAA Hall of Champions
One NCAA Plaza
700 West Washington
Indianapolis, IN 46204
http://www.ncaa.org/hall_of_champions/global/home.htm

Naismith Memorial Basketball Hall of Fame
1000 West Columbus Avenue
Springfield, MA 01105
413/781-6500 or 877/4HOOPLA
http://www.basketballhalloffame.com

ON THE WEB

National Basketball Association
http://www.nba.com

National Junior Basketball League
http://www.njbl.org

Women's National Basketball Association
http://www.wnba.com

Youth Basketball Association of America
http://www.yboa.org

INDEX

ABOUT THE AUTHOR

Brian Eule lives in California. He is a graduate of Stanford University. His writing has appeared in several magazines and daily newspapers including *Living Well*, *Stanford Magazine*, the *San Jose Mercury News*, the *Arizona Republic*, the *Colorado Springs Gazette*, the *Arkansas Democrat-Gazette* and *Basketball America*, among others. This is his first book.